LIGHTNING BOLT BOOKS™

How Big? How Heavy? How Dense?
A Look at Matter

Jennifer Boothroyd

Lerner Publications Company

Minneapolis

J 530 Boo
588
Oct.19/11
C.1

For Gloria,
whose friendship
matters to me

Copyright © 2011 by Lerner Publishing Group, Inc.

All rights reserved. International copyright secured. No part of this book may be reproduced,
stored in a retrieval system, or transmitted in any form or by any means—electronic, mechanical,
photocopying, recording, or otherwise—without the prior written permission of Lerner Publishing
Group, Inc., except for the inclusion of brief quotations in an acknowledged review.

Lerner Publications Company
A division of Lerner Publishing Group, Inc.
241 First Avenue North
Minneapolis, MN 55401 U.S.A.

Website address: www.lernerbooks.com

Library of Congress Cataloging-in-Publication Data

Boothroyd, Jennifer, 1972–
    How big? how heavy? how dense? : a look at matter / by Jennifer Boothroyd.
        p.   cm. — (Lightning bolt books™ — Exploring physical science)
    Includes index.
    ISBN 978-0-7613-6095-7 (lib. bdg. : alk. paper)
    1. Matter—Juvenile literature. I. Title.
    QC173.16.B66 2011
    530—dc22   2010008079

Manufactured in the United States of America
1 — CG — 12/31/10

Newmarket Public Library

Contents

What Is Matter?

Matter is everywhere in the universe.

Matter is anything that has mass and volume. Mass is the amount of material in an object. Volume is the amount of space an object takes up.

This bird has mass and volume. So does its nest.

Matter can be living. Plants are matter. People are matter. Animals and bugs are matter.

Matter can be nonliving. Air is matter. Your favorite jacket is matter.

Things you cannot see, like air, can be matter. But the sound of blowing wind isn't matter. That's because it doesn't take up space.

Properties of Matter

All matter has properties. Properties describe how matter looks, feels, or acts. Color, texture, shape, size, and weight are all properties.

What are some properties of this starfish?

Matter is sorted by its properties. Matter can be sorted by color.

The red apples and green apples are in different bins.

Matter can be

sorted by texture.

This sandpaper feels rough. Cotton (top) feels soft.

Matter can be sorted by shape or size.

Clothes come in different sizes.

Matter can be sorted by weight.

The rocks (left) are heavier than the feathers (right).

Matter can be sorted by density. Density is how heavy something is for its size.

A baseball is heavy for its size. It is dense.

A ball of yarn is light for its size. It is not very dense.

Matter also can be sorted by what it's made of. The bottle on the right is made of glass. The bottle on the left is made of plastic.

Matter with certain properties works best for certain tasks. Would flimsy or solid matter make a better floor for a tree house?

Would hard or soft matter make better stuffing for a pillow?

Forms of Matter

Matter comes in three forms.

The three forms of matter are solid, liquid, and gas.

A mug is a solid.
Cocoa is a liquid.
Steam is a gas.

Solids hold one shape. You cannot pour them. They will not spread to fill a space.

These rocks are solids. They cannot be poured. If you put them in a pail, they would keep their shape.

Liquids don't hold their shape. They can be poured. They will spread to fill a space.

Water is a liquid. You can pour it. If you put it in a pail, it will take on the pail's shape.

Gases don't hold their shape.
Unlike liquids, you cannot
pour them. But like liquids,
they will spread to fill a space.

Air is a gas. You cannot
pour it. Air spreads to fill
the space inside the pail.

Changing Matter

Matter can change its form when it is heated or cooled.

Ice cream is a solid.
It melts when
it gets warm.
It becomes
a liquid.

Juice is a liquid. It freezes
when it gets cold.

It becomes a solid.

Liquid water changes to steam when it gets hot. It becomes a gas called water vapor.

Water vapor rises from the surface of a lake.

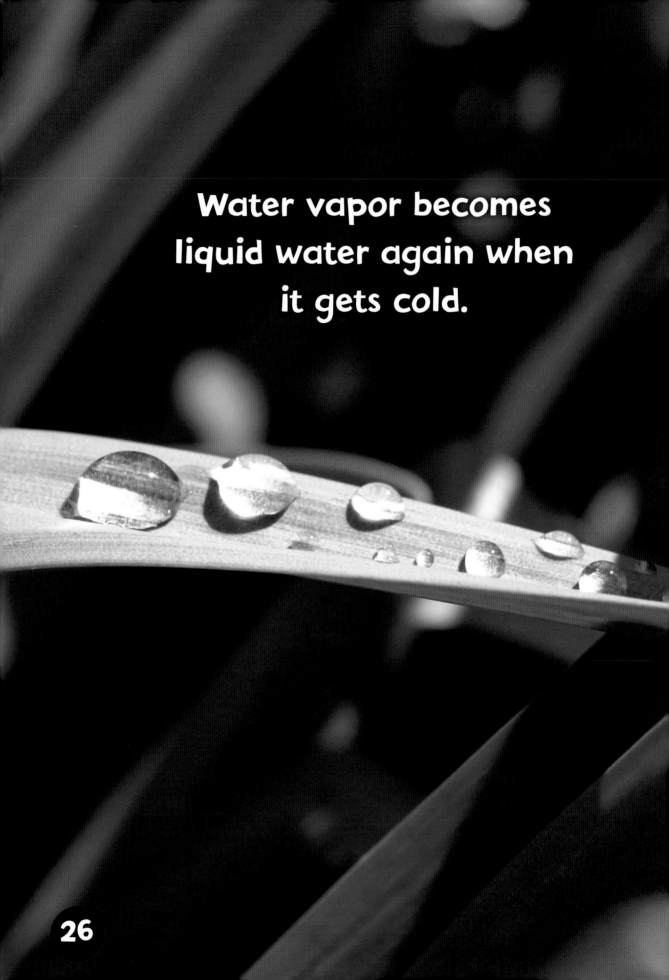

Water vapor becomes
liquid water again when
it gets cold.

Matter makes life possible.

Activity

Invisible Matter

You can't see air. But you can prove that it takes up space. Give this fun experiment a try!

What you need:

a balloon

a two-liter plastic soda bottle

What you do:

1. Blow up the balloon. Then let all the air out.
2. Put the deflated balloon inside the bottle. Wrap the lip of the balloon over the bottle's rim.
3. Holding the bottle, blow into the balloon. Stop if you feel light-headed.

Is it hard to inflate the balloon? That's because there is air in the bottle. When you wrapped the balloon around the bottle's rim, the air became sealed inside the bottle. Normally when you blow up a balloon, the air around the balloon moves out of the way as the balloon gets bigger. But the air inside the bottle couldn't move out of the way. It stopped you from making the balloon bigger.

Glossary

density: how heavy something is for its size

gas: a substance that will spread to fill any space that contains it

liquid: a wet substance that you can pour

mass: the amount of material in an object

matter: anything that has mass and volume

property: a quality or characteristic of something. Properties describe how matter looks, feels, or acts.

solid: something that is hard and firm and is neither a liquid nor a gas

volume: the amount of space an object takes up

water vapor: the gas produced when water changes to steam

Further Reading

BBC Schools Science Clips: Grouping and Changing Materials
http://www.bbc.co.uk/schools/scienceclips/ages/6_7/grouping_materials.shtml

Boothroyd, Jennifer. *Many Kinds of Matter: A Look at Solids, Liquids, and Gases.* Minneapolis: Lerner Publications Company, 2011.

Dragonfly TV: Matter and Motion
http://pbskids.org/dragonflytv/show/mattermotion.html

Gifford, Clive. *Materials.* Boston: Kingfisher, 2005.

Murray, Julie. *Matter.* Edina, MN: Abdo, 2007.

Index

Photo Acknowledgments

The images in this book are used with the permission of: © Azurviews/Dreamstime .com, p. 1; © Dyscoh/Dreamstime.com, p. 2; Photo courtesy of NASA/JPL, p. 4; © William Leaman/Alamy, p. 5; © iStockphoto.com/Lise Gagne, p. 6; © SuperStock Creative/SuperStock, p. 7; © DEA/P. Jaccod/De Agostini/Getty Images, p. 8; © McConnell & McNamara/StockFood Creative/Getty Images, p. 9; © iStockphoto.com/ Floortje, p. 10 (top); © John Henkel/Shutterstock Images, p. 10 (bottom); © Jose Luis Pelaez, Inc/Blend Images/Getty Images, p. 11; © Tim Ridley/Dorling Kindersley/Getty Images, p. 12; © Serna/Dreamstime.com, p. 13 (bottom); © Alex Staroseltsev/ Shutterstock Images, p. 13 (top); © EuToch/Shutterstock Images, p. 14 (right); © nilo/ Shutterstock Images, p. 14 (left); © Martin Barraud/Stone/Getty Images, p. 15; © Caroline Woodham/Digital Vision/Getty Images, p. 16; © iStockphoto.com/Al Parrish, p. 17 (top); © Tom Grill/Iconica/Getty Images, p. 17 (bottom left); © Elena Elisseeva/ Dreamstime.com, p. 17 (right); © Don Farrall/Photodisc/Getty Images, p. 18; © Zia Soleil/Iconica/Getty Images, p. 19; © Purestock/Getty Images, p. 20; © Nancypics/ Dreamstime.com, p. 21; © iStockphoto.com/Todd Gerber, p. 22; © Blend Images/Annika Erickson/Getty Images, p. 23; © Armstrong Studios/ FoodPix/Getty Images, p. 24; © imagebroker/Alamy. p. 25; © Loonchild/ Dreamstime.com. p. 26; © Stephen Simpson/SuperStock, p. 27; © Alphababy/Dreamstime.com. p. 28 (left); © Jckca/ Dreamstime.com, p. 28 (right); © Sneekerp/Dreamstime.com. p. 30; Antestio/ Dreamstime.com. p. 31.

Front cover: © Ariel Skelley/Blend Images RF/Photolibrary.